Immigration to the United States

Africans in America

Richard Worth

Robert Asher, Ph.D., General Editor

☑️®

Facts On File, Inc.

Immigration to the United States: Africans in America

Copyright © 2005 by Facts On File, Inc.

Facts On File, Inc.
132 West 31st Street
New York NY 10001

Library of Congress Cataloging-in-Publication Data
Worth, Richard.
   Africans in America / Richard Worth.
      p. cm. − (Immigration to the United States)
   Includes bibliographical references and index.
   ISBN 0-8160-5691-9
   1. African Americans−History−Juvenile literature. 2. Slaves−United States−
   History−Juvenile literature. 3. Slave trade−United States−History−Juvenile literature.
   4. Slavery−United States−History−Juvenile literature. 5. African Americans−
   Juvenile literature. I. Title. II. Series.
   E185.W93 2005
   304.8'7306−dc22

                                                                      2004014299

Facts On File books are available at special discounts when purchased in bulk quantities for businesses, associations, institutions, or sales promotions. Please call our Special Sales Department in New York at (212) 967-8800 or (800) 322-8755.

You can find Facts On File on the World Wide Web at http://www.factsonfile.com

Cover design by Cathy Rincon
A Creative Media Applications Production
Interior design: Fabia Wargin & Luís Leon
Editor: Laura Walsh
Copy editor: Laurie Lieb
Proofreader: Tania Bissell
Photo researcher: Jennifer Bright

Photo Credits:
p. 1 © AP Photo/Matthew Cavanaugh; p. 4 © AP Photo; p. 11 © Getty Images/Hulton Archive; p. 15 © Getty Images/Hulton Archive; p. 21 © CORBIS; p. 22 © Getty Images/Hulton Archive; p. 27 © CORBIS; p. 31 © Historical Picture Archive/CORBIS; p. 33 © CORBIS; p. 35 © Leonard de Selva/CORBIS; p. 39 © CORBIS; p. 43 © CORBIS; p. 45 © Getty Images/Hulton Archive; p. 48 © CORBIS; p. 53 © Bettmann/CORBIS; p. 55 © CORBIS; p. 59 © Bettmann/CORBIS; p. 63 © Getty Images/Hulton Archive; p. 66 © Oscar White/CORBIS; p. 69 © CORBIS; p. 71 © Hulton-Deutsch Collection/CORBIS; p. 73 © Bettmann/CORBIS; p. 77 © Bettmann/CORBIS; p. 79 © AP Photo; p. 81 © AP Photo/James A. Finley; p. 84 © AP Photo/Michael Schmelling; p. 87 © AP Photo/Michael Dwyer; p. 88 © Reuters/CORBIS

Printed in the United States of America

VH PKG 10 9 8 7 6 5 4 3 2 1

This book is printed on acid-free paper.

Previous page: *The Conto family of Tacoma Park, Maryland, are recent immigrants from Liberia.*

Contents

A Nation of Immigrants

Robert Asher, Ph.D.

Human beings have always moved from one place to another. Sometimes they have sought territory with more food or better economic conditions. Sometimes they have moved to escape poverty or been forced to flee from invaders who have taken over their territory. When people leave one country or region to settle in another, their movement is called emigration. When people come into a new country or region to settle, it is called immigration. The new arrivals are called immigrants.

People move from their home country to settle in a new land for two underlying reasons. The first reason is that negative conditions in their native land push them to leave. These are called "push factors." People are pushed to emigrate from their native land or region by such things as poverty, religious persecution, or political oppression.

The second reason that people emigrate is that positive conditions in the new country pull them to the new land. These are called "pull factors." People immigrate to new countries seeking opportunities that do not exist in their native country. Push and pull factors often work together. People leave poor conditions in one country seeking better conditions in another.

Sometimes people are forced to flee their homeland because of extreme hardship, war, or oppression. These immigrants to new lands are called refugees. During times of war or famine, large groups of refugees may immigrate to new countries in search of better conditions. Refugees have been on the move from the earliest recorded history. Even today, groups of refugees are forced to move from one country to another.

Pulled to America

For hundreds of years, people have been pulled to America seeking freedom and economic opportunity. America has always been a land of immigrants. The original settlers of America emigrated from Asia thousands of years ago. These first Americans were probably following animal herds in search of better hunting grounds. They migrated to America across a land bridge that connected the west coast of North America with Asia. As time passed, they spread throughout North and South America and established complex societies and cultures.

Beginning in the 1500s, a new group of immigrants came to America from Europe. The first European immigrants to America were volunteer sailors and soldiers who were promised rewards for their labor. Once settlements were established, small numbers of immigrants from Spain, Portugal, France, Holland, and England began to arrive. Some were rich, but most were poor. Most of these emigrants had to pay for the expensive ocean voyage from Europe to the Western Hemisphere by promising to work for four to seven years. They were called indentured servants. These emigrants were pushed out of Europe by religious persecution, high land prices, and poverty. They were pulled to America by reports of cheap, fertile land and by the promise of more religious freedom than they had in their homelands.

Many immigrants who arrived in America, however, did not come by choice. Convicts were forcibly transported from England to work in the American colonies. In addition, thousands of African men, women, and children were kidnapped in Africa and forced onto slave ships. They were transported to America and forced to work for European masters. While voluntary emigrants had some choice of which territory they would move to, involuntary immigrants had no choice at all. Slaves were forced to immigrate to America from the 1500s until about 1840. For voluntary immigrants, two things influenced where they settled once they arrived in the United States. First, immigrants usually settled where there were jobs. Second, they often settled in the same places as immigrants who had come before them, especially those who were relatives or who had come from the same village or town in their homeland. This is called chain migration. Immigrants felt more comfortable living among people whose language they understood and whom they might have known in the "old country."

Immigrants often came to America with particular skills that they had learned in their native countries. These included occupations such as carpentry, butchering, jewelry making, metal machining, and farming. Immigrants settled in places where they could find jobs using these skills.

In addition to skills, immigrant groups brought their languages, religions, and customs with them to the new land. Each of these many cultures has made unique contributions to American life. Each group has added to the multicultural society that is America today.

Waves of Immigration

Many immigrant groups came to America in waves. In the early 1800s, economic conditions in Europe were growing harsh. Famine in Ireland led to a massive push of emigration of Irish men and women to the United States. A similar number of

German farmers and urban workers migrated to America. They were attracted by high wages, a growing number of jobs, and low land prices. Starting in 1880, huge numbers of people in southern and eastern Europe, including Italians, Russians, Poles, and Greeks, were facing rising populations and poor economies. To escape these conditions, they chose to immigrate to the United States. In the first 10 years of the 20th century, immigration from Europe was in the millions each year, with a peak of 8 million immigrants in 1910. In the 1930s, thousands of Jewish immigrants fled religious persecution in Nazi Germany and came to America.

Becoming a Legal Immigrant

There were few limits on the number of immigrants that could come to America until 1924. That year, Congress limited immigration to the United States to only 100,000 per year. In 1965, the number of immigrants allowed into the United States each year was raised from 100,000 to 290,000. In 1986, Congress further relaxed immigration rules, especially for immigrants from Cuba and Haiti. The new law allowed 1.5 million legal immigrants to enter the United States in 1990. Since then, more than half a million people have legally immigrated to the United States each year.

Not everyone who wants to immigrate to the United States is allowed to do so. The number of people from other countries who may immigrate to America is determined by a federal law called the Immigration and Naturalization Act (INA). This law was first passed in 1952. It has been amended (changed) many times since then.

Following the terrorist attacks on the World Trade Center in New York City and the Pentagon in Washington, D.C., in 2001, Congress made significant changes in the INA. One important change was to make the agency that administers laws concerning immigrants and other people entering the United States part of the Department of Homeland Security (DHS). The DHS is responsible for protecting the United States from attacks by terrorists. The new immigration agency is called the Citizenship and Immigration Service (CIS). It replaced the previous agency, which was called the Immigration and Naturalization Service (INS).

When noncitizens enter the United States, they must obtain official permission from the government to stay in the country. This permission is called a visa. Visas are issued by the CIS for a specific time period. In order to remain in the country permanently, an immigrant must obtain a permanent resident visa, also called a green card. This document allows a person to live, work, and study in the United States for an unlimited amount of time.

To qualify for a green card, an immigrant must have a sponsor. In most cases, a sponsor is a member of the immigrant's family who is a U.S. citizen or holds a green card. The government sets an annual limit of 226,000 on the number of family members who may be sponsored for permanent residence. In addition, no more than 25,650 immigrants may come from any one country.

In addition to family members, there are two other main avenues to obtaining a green card. A person may be sponsored by a U.S. employer or may enter the Green Card Lottery. An employer may sponsor a person who has unique work qualifications. The Green Card Lottery randomly selects 50,000 winners each year to receive green cards. Applicants for the lottery may be from any country from which immigration is allowed by U.S. law.

However, a green card does not grant an immigrant U.S. citizenship. Many immigrants have chosen to become citizens of the United States. Legal immigrants who have lived in the United States for at least five years and who meet other requirements may apply to become naturalized citizens. Once these immigrants qualify for citizenship, they become full-fledged citizens and have all the rights, privileges, and obligations of other U.S. citizens.

Even with these newer laws, there are always more people who want to immigrate to the United States than are allowed by law. As a result, some people choose to come to the United States illegally. Illegal immigrants do not have permission from the U.S. government to enter the country. Since 1980, the number of illegal immigrants entering the United States, especially from Central and South America, has increased greatly. These illegal immigrants are pushed by poverty in their homelands and pulled by the hope of a better life in the United States. Illegal immigration cannot be exactly measured, but it is believed that between 1 million and 3 million illegal immigrants enter the United States each year.

Right: A group of Nigerian tribal dancers perform in traditional costumes in 1956. Nigeria is one of more than 50 countries that make up Sub-Saharan Africa.

This series, Immigration to the United States, describes the history of the immigrant groups that have come to the United States. Some came because of the pull of America and the hope of a better life. Others were pushed out of their homelands. Still others were forced to immigrate as slaves. Whatever the reasons for their arrival, each group has a unique story and has made a unique contribution to the American way of life.

A Unique Story of Immigration

Africa

Africa is the second-largest continent on Earth. It stretches for almost 5,000 miles (8,000 km) from north to south and equals about 23 percent of the world's total landmass. Modern Africa is made up of about 50 countries and is home to about 800 million people. Many scientists believe that the first human beings appeared in Africa between 5 and 2 million years ago. These first humans later spread from Africa throughout the world. If this is true, the first immigrants were Africans.

Because of its geographical makeup, the countries of Africa are often divided into two groups. The Sahara Desert, the largest desert in the world, stretches across the northern part of the continent and separates the two Africas. North Africa is made up of the countries north of the Sahara Desert. These are Algeria, Egypt, Libya, Morocco, Tunisia, and

Western Sahara. Historically and culturally, these countries are very different from those in the south. Most people in North Africa are Muslims and in general, North African countries are more prosperous than those to the south are.

Below the Sahara Desert lies the region known as Sub-Saharan Africa. It is made up of many countries, cultures, and religious groups. Eighty percent of Africa's population lives south of the Sahara Desert. Most Africans who have come to America during the past 400 years, including almost all those brought to America as slaves, came from this region. This book traces the journey of Sub-Saharan Africans to America and describes their lives in their new land.

Becoming African Americans

The story of Africans coming to America is not like that of any other immigrant group. Unlike other immigrant groups, most Africans did not come to America by choice. They were kidnapped, enslaved, and brought to North America against their will. From the early 1600s until about 1800, millions of African slaves were brought to America. The story of Africans in America is primarily the story of these involuntary immigrants and their descendants.

Very few Africans immigrated to the United States voluntarily until the last part of the 20th century. The existence of slavery into the mid-1800s and the difficult social conditions faced by blacks in the United States well into the 20th century made the country inhospitable to Africans. While some Africans may have been pushed to emigrate by economic and political conditions in their countries, until the last decades of the 20th century very few were pulled to the United States.

In fact, before 1900, less than one in every 10,000 voluntary immigrants to the United States came from Africa. The number of voluntary African immigrants recorded by the U.S. government averaged only a few hundred per decade. Even during the early 1900s, when millions of immigrants arrived from other parts of the world, only a few thousand Africans immigrated to the United States.

The story of Africans already in the United States, meanwhile, changed dramatically as a result of the Civil War when the slaves were freed. However, African Americans still faced discrimination that often prevented them from voting, holding well-paying jobs, or getting an education that would help them compete in a white-dominated society. Despite these hardships, African Americans made important cultural contributions, especially in the areas of music and literature.

As the 20th century progressed, African Americans gained even more rights. Strengthened by support from U.S. Supreme Court decisions, African Americans, along with supporters of all races, forced the federal government to pass laws

> # It's a Fact!
>
> **Millions of Africans were brought to America as slaves from the early 1600s until slavery was abolished during the Civil War. In addition, a total of 841,068 Africans immigrated to the United States voluntarily between 1820 and 2003.**

ensuring that they received the same rights as other citizens. Even so, until 1970, Africans made up less than one percent of the total number of people who immigrated to the United States.

Since that period, immigration from Africa has continued to increase slowly. The U.S. Citizenship and Immigration service reported that approximately 49,000 people immigrated to the United States from Sub-Saharan Africa in 2003. That equals about seven percent of the 705,827 immigrants from all countries during that year. While few in number, these immigrants have introduced elements of their culture to their new country. In addition, many African-American descendants of slaves have reached back to African traditions and culture to enrich their lives.

Many recent African immigrants along with the descendants of enslaved Africans have achieved the education, employment, and social status that have put them on an equal footing with white Americans. Even so, many African Americans live in poverty and experience discrimination. This is a reminder of how far African Americans still must travel although as a group they have lived in North America for almost four centuries.

Opposite: *This illustration dated 1774 shows a slave in chains and illustrates the inhumanity of slavery with the words "Am I not a man and a brother?" Some white Americans in the 1700s thought slavery was wrong even though Africans would be brought to America as slaves legally until 1808.*

Chapter One

The First African Americans

Involuntary Immigrants

Africans in the New World

On a summer day in 1619, a Dutch merchant ship appeared outside the harbor at Jamestown, Virginia. The ship carried 20 black Africans. Unlike the English settlers who had come to Virginia, these immigrants had not come by choice. They had been captured in western Africa, forced onto the Dutch ship, and brought against their will to the New World. They were the first African immigrants to arrive in North America.

"I was early snatched away from my native country, with about eighteen or twenty more boys and girls, as we were playing in a field," recalled Ottobah Cugoano. "We lived but a few days' journey from the coast where we were kidnapped. . . . Some of us attempted, in vain, to run away, but pistols and cutlasses [swords] were soon introduced, threatening, that if we offered to stir, we should all lie dead on the spot."

Sub-Saharan
Africa

Ottobah Cugoano's story was similar to the experience of many Africans who were sold into slavery. During the 15th century, Portuguese merchants had established trading stations on the western coast of Africa. They traded jewelry, colorful calico cloth, and other items with local African tribes for slaves. These men, women, and even children, like Ottobah Cugoano, were often captured during tribal warfare. They were then roped together, transported to the coast, and sold to Portuguese merchants.

By the early 16th century, there was a large demand for slaves in the New World. In the 1490s, Christopher Columbus had sailed to the islands of the Caribbean Sea under the flag of Spain. During his voyages, Columbus landed on several islands, which he named San Salvador, Guadeloupe, Dominica, and Hispaniola. The native population that Columbus met on these islands was a peaceful people known as the Arawak.

The Spaniards rapidly established a colony on the island of Hispaniola, laying out towns and huge farms called plantations. Instead of working the plantations themselves or paying workers, they enslaved the local Arawak, forcing them to plant and harvest the crops. The Arawak became slaves on the Spanish plantations.

During their contact with the Spanish, the Arawak also were exposed to European diseases. The Arawak had no resistance to diseases such as smallpox and measles, and many of them died. As a result, the Spanish no longer had enough slaves to work their farms, and so they began to import them from Africa.

The First American Slaves

During the 16th century, Portuguese traders began to export African slaves to the New World. The first Africans worked on Spanish and Portuguese plantations in Central and South

America. Gradually other countries, including France and Holland, also began to participate in the slave trade. At first, most of the African slaves were brought to the Caribbean, but gradually a market for Africans began to develop in the English colonies of North America.

African slaves worked in the tobacco and wheat fields. When they were not working in the fields, slaves were permitted to plant their own gardens and sell the extra vegetables. Other slaves became artisans, or skilled workers, like carpenters, stonemasons, seamstresses, and cooks. When these slaves were not busy with work on their masters' plantations, they could be hired out to other plantation owners. The slaves were even permitted to keep part of the money their masters received for their work. Some slaves saved enough money to purchase their own freedom. Other slaves were freed after their owner died. As a result, communities of free African Americans arose in Maryland and Virginia.

Slaves were also brought to the northern colonies. In New Netherland, which was controlled by the Dutch, the population of settlers was small. Therefore, slaves were shipped into the colony to help farmers and artisans. By 1664, when England took control of the colony and changed its name to New York, about 20 percent of the people living in New York City were slaves. There were also slaves living in other northern cities, such as Philadelphia, Boston, and Newport, Rhode Island. Some of these slaves worked on the docks as sailors, barrel makers, or sailmakers. In addition, slaves were employed by the northern colonists in various trades, such as iron manufacturing, copper mining, and tanning animal hides into leather. Like slaves in the

It's a Fact!

According to one estimate, approximately 100,000 slaves reached the Americas, including the Caribbean and South America, between 1525 and 1575.

South, some African Americans in northern colonies earned enough money to purchase their freedom.

Slavery Grows

During the last half of the 17th century, more workers were needed in the colonies, and the number of African slaves being brought to North America increased. Many African slaves were brought to the colonies by the English Royal African Company, which was started in 1672. The company established trading posts, called factories, along the African coast. Slaves were brought to these factories by African slave catchers who captured them, chained them together in long lines called coffles, and marched them to the coast. The African slave catchers exchanged their captives for goods brought by the English and other Europeans. Describing these goods and why the Africans wanted them, one of the European slave traders said:

> *The broad linen [fabric] serves to adorn themselves. . . . The copper basins to wash and shave . . . from the iron bars the smiths forge out all their weapons and country and household tools and utensils. . . . Muskets . . . and cutlaces [swords] they use in war. Brandy is most commonly spent at their feasts.*

The Europeans, however, were shrewd traders and regularly tried to cheat the Africans by adding water to the brandy or shortening the bolts of cloth.

Once a deal had been made, the slaves were kept at a factory until a ship was ready to leave for the New World. At these factories, some of the slaves caught diseases

It's a Fact!

In the North, many slaves lived in cities. During the 17th century, 75 percent of the wealthy families in Philadelphia owned slaves, while many residents of Boston had one or two slaves to wait on them.

and died. Indeed, slaves who became sick might be murdered to prevent other Africans from being infected. After a cargo of slaves was collected, they were packed aboard the Royal African Company's sailing ships and brought to English colonies in the Caribbean and North America.

For the Africans, the journey from their homes was a brutal experience. Many of them were so upset at leaving Africa and at their dismal future that they jumped into the sea and drowned themselves. Others became so depressed that they refused to eat. They sometimes starved to death before reaching America.

In the Slave Trade

A sailor named John Barbot worked in the slave trade during the late 17th century. As Barbot explained, the slaves brought from the interior of Africa were "put into a booth, or prison, built for that purpose, near the beach." Then they were examined by the European traders, and those who seemed fit were purchased and "marked on the breast, with a red-hot iron, imprinting the mark of the French, English, or Dutch companies." Eventually, the slaves were loaded on board a ship to be taken to the New World. However, they often resisted their captors and refused to eat on the ship. As Barbot explained, sometimes he caused "the teeth of those wretches to be broken, because they would not open their mouths . . . and thus have forced some sustenance into their throats." Once Barbot was attacked during a slave revolt aboard his ship. Although the slaves killed the ship's cook and wounded several sailors, the revolt was finally put down. Twenty to 30 slaves either were killed or jumped overboard and drowned.

The slaves' journey across the Atlantic Ocean in a sailing ship was called the Middle Passage. The Africans were forced below deck in an area so cramped that they could not stand up. They were forced to lie on their sides. They were chained together, so many of them could not reach the tubs that had been placed in their quarters to be used as toilets. The smell below decks was terrible, and the human wastes became a breeding ground for fatal diseases. A slave named Zamba Zembola, who was captured and carried across the Atlantic during the 18th century, later described his ordeal. "After being about 15 days out to sea," he wrote,

> *A heavy squall [storm] struck the ship. The poor slaves below, altogether unprepared for such an occurrence, were mostly thrown to the side, where they lay heaped on the top of each other; their [chains] rendered many of them helpless, and before they could be arranged in their proper places and relieved from their pressure on each other, it was found that 15 of them were smothered or crushed to death.*

The slave traders tried to prevent too many Africans from dying because the losses reduced the amount of money the traders would make from the sale of the slaves in the New World. The slaves were brought up on deck and fed twice a day. Their captors also forced them to dance on deck to preserve the strength of their bodies. The slaves sang very sad songs, recalling their lives in African villages. Many slaves did die, however, both from disease and by jumping overboard. Between 5 and 20 percent of African immigrants died during the Middle Passage and never reached America.

African slaves were treated cruelly aboard slave ships and crowded into cramped, dirty quarters during the long voyage.

*When African slaves arrived in America, they were displayed and sold
to their future owners at slave markets.*

Forced Immigration

O nce the surviving Africans arrived in North America, they
were sold to white settlers at ports in the North and South.
Among the busiest northern slave markets were Boston, New
York City, and Bristol, Rhode Island. By far the biggest slave
market in the South was located at Charles Town (present-day
Charleston), South Carolina. The slave ships were required to
stop outside Charles Town harbor, where the slaves were examined to make sure they carried no diseases into the colony. Once
they had passed this test, they might be sold right off the ships
to planters who were rowed out into the harbor to make their

purchases. Other slaves were brought into the city and sold at auction houses.

Planters came to Charles Town from as far south as Florida to bid at the auctions for slaves to work on their plantations. The majority of these slaves were men, who could do the backbreaking work of planting, weeding, and harvesting crops. In addition to working in the fields, slaves also learned other skills that were necessary on the plantation. Some African men became carpenters, blacksmiths, or coach drivers for their masters. Women often worked in the master's house as cooks and house cleaners. They also served as nannies for the children of the plantation owner.

During the 18th century, the demand for slaves continued to increase especially in the South as the number of plantations expanded. Throughout the thirteen colonies, slavery had become a part of everyday life. As a result, more and more Africans were brought to America as slaves.

Slave Life

From 1700 to 1770, the number of slaves in the North grew from about 5,000 to 47,000, or 4 percent of the entire population. In the South, the enslaved population increased from about 24,000 to more than 400,000. In some areas, more than 50 percent of the population was slaves. Slaves were necessary to the southern economy, which depended on the tobacco, rice, and indigo crops from large plantations. In the North, by contrast, most settlers were small farmers who tilled their own soil. Most northern farmers did not own slaves. However, many middle-class and wealthy merchants had slaves as domestic, or household, help.

To control their large black populations, some colonies passed slave codes, or laws, that greatly restricted the lives of Africans. According to the codes, slaves were not permitted to learn to read or write. To prevent them from planning a rebellion, they were forbidden to assemble together. They needed passes, signed by their white masters, to travel from one plantation to another. Colonial laws also made it very difficult for masters to free their slaves. These laws locked most African Americans into lives of perpetual slavery. Finally, plantation owners had the power to treat their slaves as brutally as they wished. Slaves had none of the human rights that white immigrants to America were likely to enjoy.

Harsh Codes

In 1707, Virginia planter Robert Carter received permission from the local court to cut off the toes of two of his slaves, who had disobeyed him. While other planters may not have been this harsh, most regarded their slaves as property. Slaves could be beaten, bought, and sold whenever it seemed necessary. If slaves managed to escape, they were often harshly treated when recaptured. The Virginia slave code stated: "whereas many times slaves run away . . . if the slave does not immediately return, anyone whatsoever may kill or destroy such slaves." A slave who was caught could be punished "by dismembering [removing the arms or legs], or in any other way."

In spite of the hardships within this highly restricted environment, African Americans developed their own rich culture that was separate from that of their white masters. As the slave population grew, more African Americans started families. On some large plantations, extended family groups of parents, children, and their relatives lived in the slave quarters near the master's house. These quarters usually consisted of small one- or two-room cabins with fireplaces where the slaves cooked their meals. The cabins were hot in the summer and, despite the fireplaces, cold during the winters. Slaves received food from their masters, such as corn, grain, and occasionally some meat. However, the quantity of food was often far from adequate to feed them properly. Slaves supplemented their diets with whatever vegetables they were permitted to grow, or by sneaking into the woods to hunt wild turkeys and other animals. They hunted without the permission of their masters, because hunting was not allowed for slaves.

Within the slave quarters, women usually married young and began having children right away. Women often had as many as eight children. When a child was born, the family brought the other slaves together for a naming ceremony, frequently giving the child the same name as a relative. Slaves often used their own African names, such as Quasho Quando, although their masters generally gave them different ones, such as Ben or Sarah. This was one of the ways that white plantation owners tried to control the lives of their slaves.

The fact that many slaves had two names (the one they received at a naming ceremony and another given to them by their masters) was an indication of the mix of African and American traditions that formed the slave culture. Slaves from various parts of Africa spoke a variety of languages. As slaves worked together in North America, these languages were blended together while the slaves also learned English. The language used by the slaves was called pidgin English—a combination of African and English words.

The religion of African Americans was a mixture of Christianity, adopted from their masters, and traditional African beliefs. For example, slaves believed that nature was full of spirits and that evil spirits could put curses on people. These curses could be removed only by a medicine man or woman. Slaves were also careful to give those who died proper burials so the spirits of the deceased would not roam the world, causing trouble for the living.

Maroons

The term *maroon* was used to describe runaway slaves who established their own communities. One of these communities was located in the Great Dismal Swamp, an area that was extremely difficult to penetrate by slave owners who wanted to recover runaway slaves. Other maroon communities were established in western North Carolina and swampy areas of Florida and Georgia. Plantation owners feared that the maroons might unite with American Indian tribes and drive white settlers out of North America. However, this never occurred in a major way.

Slave Resistance

Enslaved African Americans managed to develop their own culture, including religion and language, even though their lives were severely restricted by slavery. This was important because it meant that they were not just living as victims of this cruel system. In other words, even though they were not free, African Americans resisted slavery by worshipping and speaking in their own way. Slaves also found many other ways to resist the will of their masters. Some worked slowly, refusing to do as much work as their masters desired. Others pretended not to understand what they were supposed to do. Slaves also escaped from the plantations, sometimes heading west to the frontier where they could live in freedom. In addition to this type of rebellion, some slaves actually rebelled against the white colonists.

Opposite: *Peter Salem, a freed slave, was a soldier in the Patriot army during the Revolutionary War. He shot and killed the leader of the British forces at the Battle of Bunker Hill.*

Chapter Two

Freedom for Some, But Not All

Slavery in the United States

Independence for a Few

On a hot July day in 1776 at Philadelphia, Pennsylvania, the delegates meeting at the Second Continental Congress issued the Declaration of Independence, proclaiming the freedom of the American colonies from England. Perhaps the most important phrase in that declaration was that "all men are created equal." However, this phrase was not intended to apply to slaves. In fact, some of the founding fathers were themselves slave holders, including Thomas Jefferson and Arthur Middleton, signers of the Declaration of Independence, and George Washington, commander-in-chief of the colonies' Continental army.

It's a Fact!

In 1775, Lord Dunmore, the British colonial governor of Virginia, offered freedom to any slave, male or female, who would work for the British cause. About 300 slaves joined Dunmore's army.

Several colonies, however, took the words of the Declaration to apply to everyone. For example, Vermont, New Hampshire, and Massachusetts, each with a small number of slaves, freed them as a result. In the larger slave-holding states of the North, such as New York, Pennsylvania, and New Jersey, no steps were taken to free slaves.

During the War

Many slaves did not wait to be set free but ran away to find for themselves the freedom that was proclaimed in the Declaration of Independence. Some African Americans in the North found freedom among the British, who captured New

York City in 1776 and Philadelphia the following year. The British offered slaves their freedom as a way of turning them against the American war effort. Hundreds of slaves fled to New York and Philadelphia, where they were employed by the British building fortifications, serving on ships, and working as servants to British soldiers.

In the South, slaves also escaped from the plantations and joined the British army. In 1778, the British invaded the South, capturing Savannah, Georgia. The following year, they captured Charles Town, South Carolina. Throughout much of the South, a civil war also raged between Patriots and Loyalists, or those remaining loyal to the British. With opposing militia groups moving back and forth through the Carolinas, plantation owners often feared for their lives. Many slaves, whose masters were preoccupied with the war and the defense of their plantations, took the opportunity to escape. They poured into Savannah and Charles Town, seeking freedom in the British army. Others fought for the American army, often serving as substitutes for their masters, who were allowed to send someone to serve in their place. Still other slaves joined bands of robbers and attacked plantations.

African Americans in the Patriot Army

African Americans played an important role in the American army during the Revolutionary War. In the North, the Continental army, as the American army was known, recruited free black citizens to serve. It even decided to enlist slaves. Slave owners had to give their permission to let their slaves enlist in the army, but they were paid for the loss of their slaves. In the South, there was strong opposition to recruiting slaves. The Continental Congress tried to convince the southern colonies to accept African-American regiments and to free these slaves at the end of the war, but southern leaders opposed this idea.

By the war's end, the plantation owners had lost many of their slaves. In October 1781, the British were forced to surrender at Yorktown, Virginia, by a combined American and French army. Afterward, when the British army returned to England, they took as many as 5,000 former slaves with them.

After the War

Following the war, those former slaves who had enlisted in the American army to serve the Patriot cause had no intention of returning to slavery. In the cities, many of them mingled with free black artisans and dockworkers. They were often forced to take poorly paying jobs to survive.

It's a Fact!

Georgia plantation owners lost 10,000 slaves as a result of the Revolutionary War. Approximately 25,000 slaves escaped from South Carolina.

African Americans in the northern states who remained in slavery often found that their masters were in no hurry to free them. Pennsylvania, New York, and New Jersey passed laws that called for only a gradual emancipation (freeing) of slaves over several decades.

In the South, the status of African Americans varied from state to state. Virginia, for example, passed a law stating that any former slave was free if he had fought for the Patriot cause. In 1782, the Virginia legislature reversed a law that prohibited masters from freeing their slaves. As a result, the number of free blacks in the state jumped from 2,000 to 12,000 by 1790. Similar laws were passed in Maryland and Delaware. This led to an increase of more than 90 percent in the number of free African Americans in the states of the Upper South (Maryland, Virginia, and Delaware).

Slaves are shown working on a tobacco plantation in the American South during the 1700s.

Slaves on the Move

Meanwhile, the plantations of the Upper South were making a transition from growing tobacco to growing wheat. A wheat crop required fewer slaves, because there was far less weeding and hoeing to do. Therefore, plantation owners in the Upper South began to sell some of their slaves to masters in the Lower South (the Carolinas and Georgia) and the western territories of Kentucky and Tennessee.

In the Lower South, the demand for slaves continued to grow. Rice exports recovered after the war, and plantation owners also began to plant more cotton. Some took over plantations that had belonged to Loyalists who fled after the defeat of the British. Since they needed more and more slaves to work on these plantations, owners not only imported slaves from the Upper South, but were eager to increase the importation of slaves from Africa.

Slavery and the Constitution

Serious divisions existed between parts of the South as well as between the southern and the northern states in attitudes toward slavery. These divisions played a key role at the Constitutional Convention held at Philadelphia in 1787. The convention had been called by American leaders to rewrite the document that served as the first constitution of the United States, called the Articles of Confederation. Adopted during the Revolutionary War, the Articles outlined a national framework of government. They allowed only a weak central government, since American political leaders were wary of a powerful central government, like the one in England. They also were wary of a strong leader, like England's King George III. Therefore, under the Articles there was no president. Congress could not collect taxes without the consent of the states. Each of the states was free to develop its own foreign policy. The result was a bankrupt nation that could not even raise an army to defend itself.

The delegates soon discovered that instead of rewriting the Articles of Confederation, they needed to draft a whole new Constitution. However, the delegates from different states represented different interests that made agreement difficult. Small states, such as Connecticut and Rhode Island, wanted to make sure that large states, such as Pennsylvania and Virginia, did not have too much power in the new Congress. In addition, southern states wanted to ensure that northern states, some of which had already abolished slavery, would not try to impose their ways on the South. Southern delegates made it clear that if slavery were threatened, they would never approve a new constitution. Furthermore, delegates from the Lower South wanted to continue the international slave trade with Africa, which was opposed by many northern delegates. In turn, delegates from the Upper South feared that their own slave trade with the Lower South would be threatened if the slave trade with Africa continued. Finally, the delegates to the Constitutional Convention agreed to a compromise.

*George Washington is shown speaking to the Constitutional
Convention while other delegates look on.*

The states agreed to count three-fifths of the slave population in each state for the purposes of determining the number of representatives in Congress. This was called the Three-Fifths Compromise. It gave the slave states more representatives than just their white voting populations would otherwise allow. This helped balance the power of the northern states that had greater non-slave populations. Although slaves were counted for the purpose of determining the number of Congressional representatives for their state, they were not allowed to vote. The Three-Fifths Compromise did not grant slaves any additional rights. The states also agreed that the African slave trade would continue until 1808.

The Slave Trade Continues

With the decision by the delegates at the Constitutional Convention not to end the slave trade until 1808, the forced immigration of Africans continued. Over the next 20 years, South Carolina imported 90,000 slaves from Africa. Most entered through Charleston (the name had been changed from Charles Town in 1783), while others were imported through ports such as Savannah, Georgia. Over the next half-century, slavery would move westward into new states and the number of slaves would increase five-fold. Throughout the colonial period few Africans came to America voluntarily. Most Africans avoided contact with white people for fear of being enslaved. ❖

Opposite: *Slave families were sometimes kept together and sometimes separated when they were sold at slave auctions in 19th-century America.*

Chapter Three

The Growth of Slavery

A Group without Rights

Forced Migration

At the beginning of the 19th century, slaves chained together in coffles could be seen traveling with their owners out of the Upper South. They were heading for Tennessee, Kentucky, and the Mississippi Territory, which included the present-day states of Alabama and Mississippi. A forced migration of African Americans was under way, as large as the movement of slaves from Africa during the previous two centuries.

Along the way, older slaves were sold by their owners while younger and hardier African-American men and women continued the journey south and west. These slaves were strong enough to endure the exhausting work of carving out new plantations for their owners on cheap land that was available in the West and along the coast of the Gulf of Mexico. The slaves hacked down trees, built houses, and planted corn crops to feed the people who lived on the plantations. They then began to plant cotton and sugarcane.

The Demand for Slaves

In the 1790s, the production of cotton had been revolutionized by a schoolteacher from Connecticut named Eli Whitney. Whitney had invented a device called the cotton gin (*gin* was short for *engine*), which could separate seed from cotton 50 times faster than a person could do it by hand. The warm climate of Kentucky, Tennessee, Arkansas, and the states along the Gulf Coast was ideal for growing cotton. Cotton was in great demand for manufacturing clothing. Southern planters saw the opportunity to reap huge profits, and they worked their slaves hard to bring in a bountiful cotton crop. Cottonseeds were planted in the spring, and the plants were thinned during the summer. The white cotton bolls were picked in August. "It was a tedious process," wrote historian Ira Berlin, "which often continued through Christmas into the new year. It was also painful . . . as the sharp edges of the bolls cut deep gashes into the pickers' hands, slowing the work."

In southern Louisiana, planters established sugarcane plantations, where the work was even harder. Slaves cut the cane and processed it into sugar, working day and night at harvesting time. As one slave put it: "On cane plantations in sugar time, there is no distinction as to the days of the week." According to one estimate, a slave could endure only about seven years on a sugar plantation before dying from overwork.

During the 19th century, the demand for slaves grew to keep up with production on the cotton and sugar plantations. According to historian Hugh Thomas, "As many Africans were probably introduced into the United States in the last twenty years of the eighteenth century and the first eight years of the nineteenth century as in the entire era since the 1620s." From 1803 to 1807, South Carolina alone imported about 40,000 slaves. After the ban on the African slave trade took effect in 1808, slave ships continued to operate illegally.

It's a Fact!

Between 1820 and 1830, only 17 Africans came to the United States as voluntary immigrants. During this same period, more than 150,000 immigrants arrived in America from other places.

Over the next half-century, 10,000 to 20,000 slaves were brought into the United States illegally. The demand for slaves among cotton plantation owners continued to rise, and with it the price of slaves. This made the illegal slave trade very profitable.

Slave Auctions

Slave auctions were extremely demeaning for African Americans, who found themselves being examined by potential buyers as if they were animals. As one observer reported:

The negroes were examined with as little consideration as if they had been brutes indeed; the buyers pulling their mouths open to see their teeth, pinching their limbs to find how muscular they were, walking them up and down to detect any signs of lameness, making them stoop and bend in different ways that they might be certain [of] no concealed rupture or wound; and in addition to all this treatment, asking them scores of questions relative to their qualifications and accomplishments.

Domestic Slave Trade

Most of the slaves imported to the Lower South in the early 19th century, however, were not from Africa but transported from older plantations in Virginia and Maryland. Historians estimate that about a million slaves were transported in this way, about 20,000 per year. Planters on tobacco, wheat, and corn plantations, who no longer needed as many slaves, saw the opportunity to make a substantial profit by selling them to the cotton planters who wanted them.

Throughout the South, the business of slave trading was handled by professional dealers. They regularly placed advertisements in local newspapers seeking slaves for sale. One advertisement in Asheville, North Carolina, stated: "Negroes Wanted. We want to buy from 100 to 500 Negroes for whom we will pay the highest cash prices." Another trader in Maryland advertised for fifty "Young Negroes, of both sexes, from ten to thirty years of age. Persons wishing to dispose of slaves, would find it to their advantage to give me a call, as I feel disposed to pay the highest market price." Some slave dealers operated in major southern cities, such as Richmond, Virginia.

Historians estimate that one in three slave families was separated by sale, and that about 20 percent of children under the age of 14 were taken from their parents. This was one of the most horrifying aspects of slavery. Slaves lived under the constant fear that their families might be destroyed by sales. White masters rationalized the breakup of slave families by insisting that African Americans did not regard their family relationships in the same way as whites did and that it made no difference to African Americans if they lost their spouse or children. As one white master in Kentucky told a slave just after the slave's wife was sold, "Don't worry, you can get another one."

Slaves are shown using a cotton gin. This machine helped dramatically increase the need for slaves throughout the South.

New Lives

Once they reached their destination on another plantation, slaves were regularly accepted into new adoptive families. Young slaves grew up, courted, and eventually married. Slaves needed the permission of their masters to marry, although a slave marriage was not recognized by law in the southern states. The marriage ceremony was usually quite simple, consisting of Christian prayers combined with a traditional custom, like jumping over a broomstick. "Jumping the broom" was a ritual created by slaves that may have echoed a traditional wedding ritual practiced in some parts of Africa. It also symbolized "sweeping out" the old and sweeping in the new.

On average, slave women gave birth to their first child at the age of 21 and then gave birth every two years after that. Plantation owners allowed women very little time to spend with their newborn children. Women were expected to return to the fields right away after giving birth, where they worked side by side with men. One slave recalled that she "ploughed, hoed, split rails. I done the hardest work ever a man ever did." Booker T. Washington, who was born into slavery and went on to become a prominent African-American educator, said that his mother "had little time to give to the training of her children during the day. She snatched a few moments for our care in the early morning before her work began, and at night after the day work was done."

It's a Fact!

Many slaves were brought to New Orleans on boats that came down the Mississippi River. As one slave recalled, the traders "would ship boat loads at a time, buying them up 2 or 3 here, 2 or 3 there, and holding them in a jail until they had a boat load. This practice gave rise to the expression 'sold down the river.'" This phrase means that someone was abandoned or betrayed.

Very young children might be put to work inside the master's home, known by the slaves as the "great house." Sometimes children worked beside their mothers cleaning floors and polishing silver. One child, William Davis, age 6, was given the responsibility of fanning the master and his family at the dinner table to keep flies from bothering them. Even if parents did not think their children were ready for work, it was the plantation owners who decided when it was time for slave children to begin.

When they reached adolescence, many African-American children were put to work in the sugarcane or cotton fields. On large plantations, slaves regularly worked under the guidance of an overseer. Some plantation owners promoted highly productive slaves to the position of overseer, but more often slaves were promoted to the position of slave driver. The slave driver worked for the overseer and supervised the day-to-day tasks of the slaves.

Slaves who worked too slowly or did not do exactly as they were told might be whipped. Recalling her master and mistress, one slave named Ella Wilson said:

> *He would whip me on one side till that was sore and full of blood and then he would whip me on the other side till that was all tore up. I got a scar big as the place my old mis' hit me. She took a bull whip once—the bull whip had a piece of iron in the handle of it—and she got mad. She was so mad she took the whip and hit me over the head with the butt end of it, and the blood flew. It run all down my back and dripped off my heels.*

Slaves could do little to protect each other when they were beaten, because such punishment was the master's right, according to the laws of the South.

Slaves who worked for brutal plantation owners regularly found ways to get back at their masters. They broke farm implements, escaped from the plantations, and on occasion even struck back and killed their masters or overseers. Fugitive slaves were often rounded up by slave patrols and brought back to the plantations, or brought to justice in the white courts if they had killed their masters. Slave patrols were a constant presence along the roadways that connected southern plantations. The patrols rode at night looking for any slaves who might have left their plantations without a pass.

The patrols also broke up slave gatherings, including religious services, because they feared that the slaves might be planning a rebellion. As a result, slaves often held prayer meetings at secret locations in the woods. As one slave put it, we "had a hard time trying to serve God. The patrollers would break up . . . prayer meetings and whip all caught in attendance—unless, of course, a [man] saved himself in flight." White masters wanted their slaves to attend only religious services conducted by white preachers who were approved by the plantation owners. They feared that black preachers might encourage the slaves to rebel.

Hiring Out

January 1 was not only the start of a new year, but for some slaves it was a time for leaving the plantation. To earn additional money, some plantation owners hired out their slaves. The slaves went to work on other plantations, in coal mines, on the railroads, or in flour mills and tobacco factories in nearby cities.

By living away from the plantations, hired-out slaves achieved greater freedom. They were permitted to keep a small amount of the money they earned from their work. By saving this money, some slaves eventually purchased their own freedom.

This illustration from the 1800s shows a young white girl bringing food for Christmas from the plantation house to slaves living in crude slave quarters on a plantation.

For African Americans in slavery, Christian religious services became an important part of their culture. Christianity, with its promise of a better life after death, seemed to hold out hope of an alternative to slavery. At prayer meetings, slaves raised their voices in song, asking the Lord to save them.

Sunday was generally a day of rest. On Saturday night, slaves regularly held dances. As one slave recalled: "The same old fiddler played for us that played for the white folks. And could he play! When he got that old fiddle out you couldn't keep your [feet] still."

Slave Revolts

Instead of paying to be freed, other slaves tried a more violent method. During the 19th century, a few major slave revolts were attempted in the South. One such revolt was planned by Nat Turner in 1831. Turner was a slave on a farm in northern Virginia who learned to read and became a preacher. Turner believed that God had called him to lead a revolution. "I should arise and prepare myself, and slay my enemies with their own weapons," he said. On August 21, 1831, Turner and several followers attacked and killed a white family, took their guns, and began to gather a slave army from nearby farms. They also attacked other whites, killing 55 in all. The slaves were finally stopped by the local militia, which killed some of them. The militia was unable to capture Turner, who hid out for several weeks. Nevertheless, he was eventually captured, brought to trial, found guilty, and hanged on November 11, 1831.

The rebellions of the 19th century did not achieve what the slaves set out to do. Instead, the rebellions seemed to make southerners defend slavery even more. Many southerners became more determined than ever to preserve a way of life that was built on the labor of African-American slaves. Without slaves, southerners in the Lower South believed that their economy would collapse. The attitudes of southern slave-holders toward northerners who wanted to put an end to slavery would eventually lead to severe conflict. ▨

Opposite: *This group of slaves in South Carolina was left behind by their master in 1862 when he fled from the Union army during the Civil War.*

Chapter Four

Escape
to the North

*Abolition and the
Underground Railroad*

Migration North

William Lloyd Garrison was an important leader in the abolitionist movement, which worked to end slavery. Garrison, a white man, founded his abolitionist newspaper, *The Liberator,* in Boston in 1831 and two years later helped organize the American Anti-Slavery Society. Both of these were dedicated to achieving freedom for the African-American slaves in the South. When Garrison heard about Nat Turner's rebellion, he gave it overwhelming support in the *Liberator.* "The first step of the earthquake," Garrison wrote, "which is ultimately to shake down the fabric of oppression, leaving not one stone upon the other, has been made."

A young African American whom Garrison mentioned in his newspaper was a former slave named Frederick Douglass. Born near Easton, Maryland, in 1817, Douglass was the son of a white father and a black slave mother. When Douglass was still an infant, his mother was hired out by her master. From then on, Douglass saw her infrequently. "She made her journeys to see me in the night," he later wrote in his autobiography,

> *travelling the whole distance on foot, after the performance of her day's work. She was a field hand, and a whipping is the penalty of not being in the field at sunrise, unless a slave has special permission from his or her master to the contrary—a permission which they seldom get. . . . She was with me in the night. She would lie down with me, and get me to sleep, but long before I waked she was gone.*

When Douglass was still a boy, his mother died. He began working for a master named Captain Anthony under the watchful eye of an overseer named Plummer, whom Douglass described as a "savage monster" who beat the slaves horribly.

"I have often been awakened at the dawn of day," Douglass recalled, "by the most heart-rending shrieks of an . . . aunt of mine, who he used to tie up . . . and whip on her naked back till she was literally covered with blood." As a child, Douglass said he regularly went hungry and suffered from the cold because his clothes were thin and he was given no blanket.

U.S. Immigration Records

Until 1820, the U.S. government did not keep accurate records of the number of new immigrants entering the United States. Without modern methods of communication and recordkeeping, it was difficult to track exactly how many people actually immigrated to the United States in any year. Entry into the United States was much less controlled than it is today. Many ships came and went without recording the number of people who stayed in America. People could travel overland without being stopped at the borders. The U.S. government started keeping track of the number of people who immigrated to the United States in 1820. Official U.S. government records show that for the 40-year period from 1821 to 1860 more than 5 million people immigrated to the United States. Among them were only 336 voluntary African immigrants—an average of fewer than 10 per year.

Eventually Douglass was sent to a new master, a ship's carpenter named Hugh Auld, who lived in Baltimore. Auld's wife, Sophia, began to teach Douglass how to read but was soon stopped by the master, because teaching slaves to read was a violation of the slave codes. "A [slave] should know nothing but to obey his master—to do as he is told," Auld said to his wife. Nevertheless, Douglass continued learning to read on his own and also learned how to write. With this knowledge, he eventually obtained a phony pass stating that he was a free African American and left Baltimore in 1838. He journeyed north until he reached New York City and, later, New Bedford, Massachusetts.

Douglass became an ardent abolitionist, speaking through-out New England and New York. He even traveled to England to speak. In one of his most famous speeches, delivered on July 5, 1852, he said: "What to the American slave, is your 4th of July? I answer; a day that reveals to him, more than all other days in the year, the gross injustice and cruelty to which he is the constant victim." Douglass was only one of thousands of slaves who escaped from the southern states and reached the North during the first half of the 19th century.

Many of these slaves were assisted by a vast network called the Underground Railroad. This was not an actual railroad but was given that name since railroads provided most long-distance transportation at the time. The Underground Railroad consisted of a series of paths and hiding places that slaves could follow to reach freedom. The hiding places were called stations. They were usually the homes of people, called stationmasters, who were willing to risk breaking the law and going to prison in order to help the slaves escape. Others, called conductors, guided the slaves northward, sometimes as far as Canada, where there was no slavery.

Usually, the slaves moved at night to avoid capture by the slave

Harriet Tubman was a conductor on the Underground Railroad.

patrols. With the help of the conductors, the slaves knew to follow the North Star, which pointed to freedom in the North. Then they hid out by day in stations along one of the routes out of the South. Some of these routes ran from Kentucky, across the Ohio River, and into Indiana and Ohio. Another route ran from Washington, D.C., to New York City and Albany, New York. The eastern part of North Carolina was also a center of the Underground Railroad. Escaping slaves went to Albermarle Sound on the North Carolina coast, then up the Atlantic Coast to freedom.

Some slaves did not seek the help of the Underground Railroad but escaped on their own. Harriet Jacobs was one of them. Born in 1813, Jacobs grew up as a slave in North Carolina. She was eventually sold to Dr. James Norcom, who regularly abused her. When she tried to stop him, Norcom threatened to move her to his plantation and put her to work in the fields. Jacobs escaped and, for the next seven years, hid in the attic at the home of her grandmother, a free African American named Molly Horniblow. During this time, Jacobs's two children did not know where she had gone. Although Norcom sent out the slave patrols and searched for her himself, Jacobs could not be found. Eventually, with the help of a friend named Peter, Jacobs planned her escape. In 1842, Peter rowed her to a ship waiting off the coast of North Carolina, where she was hidden and taken to Philadelphia. Jacobs described her experiences in a book, *Incidents in the Life of a Slave Girl*, published in 1861. Jacobs's book was one of several firsthand accounts by former slaves that created a new type of literature in the United States.

As she wrote:

I have not written my experiences in order to attract attention to myself. I want to add my testimony to that of abler pens to convince the people of the free states what slavery really is. Only by experience can anyone realize how deep, and dark, and foul that pit of abominations.

Harriet Tubman

Harriet Ross was born in Maryland around 1820. When she was a teenager, Harriet tried to defend another slave from the wrath of an overseer. For her trouble, the overseer threw a heavy weight at her head. She suffered lasting injuries. At age 25, Ross married John Tubman, a free African American. The Tubmans lived with the constant threat that Harriet might be sold by her master and moved far away. Eventually she decided to escape to the North. With the assistance of a neighbor and several others, she reached in Philadelphia. Soon after, Tubman went to work for the Underground Railroad. Over the next ten years, she led more than 300 slaves, including members of her own family, along the road to freedom. It was a hard walk to freedom, always with the risk of being caught and returned to the plantation, where the runaways would be whipped. However, Tubman did not allow anyone to talk about, as she put it, "giving out or going back." She would not give up until everyone who accompanied her had reached what she called the "Promised Land." This was a reference from the Bible to a land where everyone's hopes and dreams are fulfilled.

Life in the North

When former slaves arrived in the North, they discovered that life there was not as they might have expected. Although slavery had been abolished, African Americans lived under a crushing burden of discrimination. Many whites disliked African Americans, believing that they were inferior and incapable of being responsible American citizens.

During the 19th century, only four New England states—Massachusetts, New Hampshire, Vermont, and Maine—permitted African Americans to vote. In other states, such as New Jersey, Pennsylvania, and Connecticut, it was against the law for African

Americans to vote. As one Pennsylvanian put it, if the state permitted African-American males to vote, "every negro in the State, worthy and worthless—degraded and debased, as nine tenths of them are, will rush to the polls in senseless and unmeaning triumph." New states admitted to the Union in the West also usually prohibited African Americans from voting. New York had one of the largest populations of African Americans of any northern state. Citizens of all races were prevented from voting there, however, unless they owned property worth $250. While this may seem like a small amount of property, it was beyond the reach of most African Americans at the time.

Although many African Americans had been trained as artisans on plantations in the South, they were forced to work at lower-paying, unskilled jobs upon reaching the northern states. White artisans refused to work with African Americans. They did not want to compete with them for the same jobs. As a result, African-American men were forced to work as porters, buggy drivers, barbers, and waiters, while women worked as cooks, dressmakers, and house cleaners. When African Americans tried to obtain the same jobs as whites, they were often met by angry protests.

African Americans also faced other types of discrimination in the North. They were required to sit in separate cars on railroads and in separate sections on steamboats. They were prohibited from eating in most restaurants and from staying in most hotels. African Americans could not even be buried in white cemeteries.

African-American children were also prevented from attending the same schools as whites. Many politicians sincerely believed that African Americans were inferior to whites and that trying to educate them was a waste of time. Separate schools for African-American children were established, but the buildings were inadequate, the equipment and supplies inferior, and the teachers underqualified.

Higher education was also unavailable to African Americans. When several abolitionists tried to set up an African-American college in New Haven, Connecticut, in 1831, they were met by a storm of protest. An even more violent reaction occurred in Canterbury, Connecticut, when Prudence Crandall, a white woman, tried to start a school for African-American girls in 1833. A town meeting of whites in Canterbury demanded that Crandall give up her plan. Crandall would not back down. "I have put my hand to the plough," she said, "and I will never no never look back." The school opened, with African-American students from Boston, New York, and other nearby cities, in attendance. However, townspeople shouted at the girls on their way to school and polluted the water in the school well. The Connecticut legislature quickly passed a bill prohibiting Crandall's school. She took the issue to court and won a decision that kept her school open. Nevertheless, the pressure from the townspeople, who even tried to set fire to the school buildings, became overwhelming. In 1834, Crandall finally closed the doors of her school and left Connecticut.

War Approaches

In 1850, the conditions faced by former slaves escaping to the North grew even worse. The U.S. Congress passed a harsh fugitive slave law. It prohibited anyone from helping escaped slaves, and it required local authorities to return a slave if presented with a certificate of ownership by the slave's master. In reaction to the new law, abolitionists were even more determined to assist slaves. They were joined by more and more northern whites, who had become opposed to the injustices of slavery and wanted to see them ended. One of these was Harriet Beecher Stowe, who had lived for several years in Cincinnati, Ohio, where many escaping slaves went after leaving the South. She also visited a plantation across the Ohio River in Kentucky. In 1853, Stowe published a novel, *Uncle Tom's Cabin,* that graphically depicted the harsh conditions of slavery in the South. Stowe's novel sold more than 300,000 copies in a year, making it a huge best seller.

This advertisement from 1859 proclaims that Uncle Tom's Cabin *is the greatest book of the age.*

Meanwhile, clashes had broken out in the western territories of Kansas and Nebraska between slaveholders and northern farmers opposed to slavery. Each side wanted to take control of the territories. The slaveholders wanted to make them new slave states, while the northerners wanted to prevent slavery in the West. In 1857, the U.S. Supreme Court made a historic decision in *Dred Scott v. Sandford*. The Court ruled that although Dred Scott, a Missouri slave, had been taken to Illinois, a free state, he was not legally a free man but still the property of his owner.

It's a Fact!

U.S. government immigration records for 1820 report that only one new immigrant from Africa came to the United States that year.

This ruling angered many northerners opposed to slavery, increasing tensions between the North and South.

In 1859, the conflict over slavery grew even worse when John Brown, a radical white abolitionist, led a raid on the federal arsenal at Harpers Ferry in Virginia (now West Virginia). Brown was joined by a small group of whites and African Americans who hoped to take the weapons stored at the arsenal and use them to start a slave revolt in the South. Brown was captured and later executed, but many people in the North considered him a hero. In the South, slaveholders feared that abolitionists such as Brown and the people in the North who supported him threatened their way of life.

By 1860, the conflict between the North and South, as well as the future of millions of African Americans, had reached a decisive point. It would soon erupt in civil war.

Opposite: *Soldiers from the 107th Colored Infantry stand guard during the Civil War. The 107th was one of many groups of African-American soldiers who fought for the Union cause.*

Chapter Five

A Divided Nation

The Civil War and Its Aftermath

Confederates and Slaves

In December 1860, South Carolina became the first state to secede from, or leave, the Union. It was soon followed by ten other southern states. These states decided to leave the Union when Abraham Lincoln was elected president of the United States. Southerners knew that Lincoln intended to stop the expansion of slavery into the West. They feared that this would slowly undermine the plantation system. In February 1861 the southern states established the Confederate States of America. They selected Jefferson Davis, a slave owner and former U.S. senator, as their president. Two months later, a Confederate army bombarded the federal stronghold at Fort Sumter in Charleston, forcing it to surrender. This battle touched off four years of bloody civil war.

African Americans reacted to the Civil War in a variety of ways. In the South, many slaves remained on the plantations. Some of them felt a loyalty to their masters and a responsibility to uphold the only way of life that they had known for generations. They knew little about the North, except what they had been told by their owners. As one slave put it: "Mrs. Harris [the slave's mistress] was hatin' the North and I was hatin' the North too. I thought the North was kind of like a spider in a dream that was goin to come and wipe away [the] house and carry me off."

Slaves also remained on the plantations because they were afraid that, if they ran away, they would be caught by the slave patrols and severely punished. During the Civil War, the slave patrols increased their watchfulness along southern roadways, looking for slaves who might plan to run away and join the Union army. Slaves were very important to the southern war effort, because they harvested wheat, corn, and other food crops that were essential to feed Confederate soldiers.

A few slaves were even armed and fought alongside white soldiers in the Confederate army. However, the Confederates were opposed to arming large numbers of slaves. They feared that armed slaves might start a revolt. Although the slaves never revolted during the Civil War, some of them did run away to join the Union army.

Slaves Join the Union Army

As the war continued, Union forces occupied larger and larger territories throughout the South, bringing them into closer contact with slaves. In 1861, the U.S. Congress passed the Confiscation Act. This law declared that any property used by southerners to support the war effort could be confiscated, or taken, by the North. This "property" included slaves. As a result, any slaves who escaped to the Union army would not be returned to their owners. Thousands escaped and sought refuge among the Union forces, while others worked as laborers in the Union army. Some former slaves joined the Union army and fought as soldiers.

Many former male slaves brought their families along with them to the Union army camps, but the Union army did not always have the supplies or the housing to properly care for former slaves or their families. These refugees were often poorly treated in the army camps; they received little food, wore tattered clothing, and lived in makeshift huts. Winters were especially severe, and some former slaves died from cold, starvation, and disease. At one camp in Kentucky, elderly former slaves, along with women and children, were ordered to leave the camp and not return. As a result, they had to find any shelter that was available. One observer reported that he found "fourteen [of them] in an old shed doorless & floorless sitting around a stick of burning wood with no food or bedding." In some ways, freedom had become even worse than slavery.

It's a Fact!

About 29,000 African Americans served in the Union navy. With their knowledge of southern waterways, many former slaves proved invaluable as pilots on Union ships.

In the North

When the Civil War broke out, many African Americans in the North wanted to join the Union army. They hoped that the Civil War would bring an end to slavery in the South, and they were eager to do their part. As Frederick Douglass put it: "Once let the black man get upon his person the brass letters 'U.S.'; let him get an eagle on his button, and a musket on his shoulder and bullets in his pocket, and there is no power on earth which can deny that he has earned the right to citizenship." However, the Lincoln administration refused at first to arm African Americans and send them into the South. Lincoln was afraid that such a move would upset slave owners in the border states, such as Missouri and Kentucky, and convince those states to join the Confederacy. For the president, the main purpose of the war was to bring the Union back together, not to free the slaves in the South.

As the war continued, Lincoln changed his mind about letting African Americans fight. The president realized that there were not enough white males volunteering for the Union army. At first, Union commanders formed black regiments of volunteers. Some of these were former slaves who had escaped from the South. Later, as Union forces occupied areas along coastal Georgia, Florida, and South Carolina, they enlisted former southern slaves into the army.

By the end of the war in 1865, the number of enlisted black soldiers was about 180,000. African-American soldiers participated in many major campaigns throughout the rest of the Civil War. About 38,000 African-American soldiers died during the war. This number represents about one out of every five Union soldiers killed in battle. A much higher percentage of black soldiers than white soldiers died in the war. One reason was that black soldiers captured in battle were often brutally treated by southerners. In 1864, after black troops defending Fort Pillow, Tennessee, had surrendered, they were massacred by Confederate soldiers. In addition, poor equipment and a lack of adequate medical treatment increased the number of casualties among African-American troops.

Colonel Robert Gould Shaw was killed as the 54th Massachusetts made its gallant charge on the Confederate army at Fort Wagner during the Civil War.

Attack on Fort Wagner

In July 1863, the 54th Massachusetts Volunteers participated in an attack on Confederate Fort Wagner in Charleston Harbor. They faced a major challenge because Fort Wagner was heavily defended. Their commanding officer, Colonel Robert Gould Shaw, led his troops in a charge toward the fort on the evening of July 18. He vowed to "take the fort or die there." The fort's guns pounded the advancing African-American troops. But they kept advancing.

In the end, the unit was driven back after losing half of its soldiers, including Shaw. Nevertheless, the attack on Fort Wagner had proven that African-American soldiers could stand up to the toughest battle conditions and fight with bravery.

Reconstruction

In spring 1865, the Confederate army surrendered, bringing an end to the Civil War. Although President Lincoln's Emancipation Proclamation had technically freed the slaves in the Confederate states as of January 1, 1863, many remained on the plantations. With the war's end, most of these former slaves seized the opportunity to leave the plantations. They sought to reunite with family members, find jobs, and simply leave the masters they hated. Some plantation owners, however, refused to tell African Americans that the war was over until they had brought in a harvest. Afterward, they were told that they were free to leave.

This sudden freedom was difficult for some former slaves. They had never before had to provide food and shelter for themselves and their families. Many former slaves lacked the resources to do anything else but stay on the plantations, and they found themselves working the fields belonging to their former owners. Others worked as sharecroppers. These farmers rented land from their former owners and paid them back with a share of the crop they raised. The plantation owners often took advantage of them. They overcharged the sharecroppers for supplies and kept them in debt.

One of the tasks of President Andrew Johnson, who replaced Abraham Lincoln after Lincoln was assassinated in April 1865, was to come up with a plan for the reconstruction of the South and of the Union as a whole. In fact, the period immediately following the Civil War was known as Reconstruction.

President Johnson did not plan to punish the former Confederate states for causing the bloody and costly war. Johnson was a southerner himself. He allowed the southern states back into the union as long as they supported the Thirteenth Amendment to the Constitution, which had been passed in 1865 to outlaw slavery. Beyond this, Johnson let white southerners run their state governments the way they chose. As a result, white political leaders passed the Black Codes. These laws replaced the slave codes, which had existed before the war.

Under the Black Codes, in some states, African Americans were not permitted to own land or to carry a weapon. They could not leave a farm and look for work somewhere else because any African American not currently working could be put in prison. These laws were extremely unfair, but they kept whites in control of African Americans throughout the South.

In response to the Black Codes, Congress passed the Civil Rights Act of 1866, declaring that African Americans had the same rights as other citizens. That same year Congress also passed the Fourteenth Amendment to the Constitution, which gave African

It's a Fact!

During the Civil War, fewer than 300 voluntary African immigrants came to the United States while thousands of African Americans fled north into Canada to escape slavery and the war.

Americans the right to vote and to run for elected offices. Finally, in 1867, troops were sent to the South to ensure that the rights of African Americans were protected.

During the late 1860s and early 1870s, African Americans in the South enjoyed increased opportunities. Some ran for political office and were elected U.S. senators and congressmen. The newly established Freedman's Bureau, set up to assist former slaves, began an effort to build schools for African Americans. The Freedman's Bureau enlisted the help of white northern women, who came into the South to teach African Americans. The bureau also established colleges in the South, including Fisk University in Nashville, Tennessee; Hampton Institute in Hampton, Virginia; and Howard University in Washington, D.C. Some African Americans also contributed money to set up new schools.

It's a Fact!

Some African Americans moved west after the Civil War. They joined many white settlers who were establishing new homes on the frontier. Some, such as Britton Johnson, became cowboys and joined cattle drives, while James Beckwourth became a fur trapper. A few, such as Cherokee Bill and Babe Fisher, became well-known gunfighters.

In the 1870s, however, interest in Reconstruction began to decline in the North. Many northerners were focused on industrial expansion, while others were settling new lands in the West. In 1872, the Freedmen's Bureau was disbanded, and five years later northern troops were withdrawn from the South. Southerners were again free to deal with African Americans without interference from the North. For about a decade after the Civil War, African Americans had enjoyed some civil rights under Reconstruction. But now many of those rights would be taken away. ▨

Opposite: *The Cotton Club in the Harlem section of New York City was a popular nightclub and a center of the African-American artistic movement known as the Harlem Renaissance in the 1920s.*

Chapter Six

Discrimination North and South

Jim Crow and Racial Hatred

Jim Crow Laws

Henry W. Grady, the editor of one of the South's leading newspapers, the *Atlanta Constitution,* spoke for a majority of southerners when he wrote in 1887: "The supremacy of the white race of the South must be maintained forever, and the domination of the negro race resisted at all hazards—because the white race is the superior race." After Reconstruction, southern states passed laws to ensure that African Americans remained in an inferior position. These were known as Jim Crow laws, after a stage character made famous during the 19th century by a white performer named Thomas Rice. The character was an elderly black man, called Jim Crow, who grinned and shuffled across the stage and showed his respect for white folks. Jim Crow laws were passed to ensure that African Americans would "know their place" and act the same as Rice's character.

It's a Fact!

In Atlanta's public school system in 1903, there were 20 schools for about 14,500 white students, and only three schools for more than 8,000 black students.

Under the Jim Crow laws, black and white people were kept separate. On trains, for example, African Americans were forced to sit in separate cars away from whites, who generally did not want to have any contact with them. Any African American who violated the Jim Crow laws was immediately corrected or punished. As a child in Memphis, Tennessee, in the 1870s, Mary Church Terrell, an African American, mistakenly sat in a railroad car reserved for whites. She was confronted by an angry conductor. "Whose little n_____ is this?" he asked crossly. Mary was immediately removed from the car and taken to the one reserved for African Americans. "I could think of nothing I had done wrong," she later wrote. "I could not understand my overwhelming sense of shame," she wrote, "as if I had been guilty of some unknown crime."

The Jim Crow laws were applied to many parts of southern society. In railroad stations, there were separate entrances marked "For White Passengers" and "For Colored Passengers." Parks, theaters, water fountains, and public toilets were marked in the same way. Some hospitals would not accept African-American patients, no matter how sick they were.

Jim Crow laws, although unfair, were upheld by the U.S. Supreme Court in a landmark decision in 1896. The case involved an African American named Homer Plessy, who had been forced to leave a railroad car for whites and sit in a blacks-only car. In *Plessy v. Ferguson,* the Supreme Court ruled that "separate but equal" facilities were legal for American citizens. As the Supreme Court explained, "If one race be inferior to the other socially, the Constitution of the United State cannot put them upon the same plane" or bring about "an enforced commingling of the two races."

Jim Crow laws also forced African-American children into separate schools that were usually inferior to white schools. In practice, "separate but equal" almost always meant separate and unequal. According to historian Leon Litwack, white political leaders did not want to educate African-American children for fear that they might no longer accept their inferior place in southern society.

Many older African Americans hesitated to step above their place in southern society, afraid of what might happen to them. They remembered all too well the whippings and other punishments they suffered during slavery. Whites regularly retaliated against African Americans who appeared to be too successful. In Georgia, African Americans who had managed to save some money and run small businesses were ordered to leave the area. One of these, a farmer, along with his two daughters, was killed

Booker T. Washington

Booker T. Washington was born into slavery in Virginia in 1856. After he was freed in 1865, Washington moved with his family to West Virginia. In 1872, he attended Hampton Institute, an African-American trade school in Virginia, graduating in 1875. When he returned four years later to teach at the institute, he was befriended by General Samuel Chapman Armstrong, the head of the school. Armstrong was so impressed with Washington that he recommended Washington to head a new school, Tuskegee Institute, in Alabama. When Washington arrived at Tuskegee, the school had very few students, who attended classes in a rundown building. Thanks to Washington's efforts, the school gradually expanded, attracting many more students.

Washington traveled throughout the United States, raising money for Tuskegee Institute and making it famous. The school taught students practical skills, such as farming and carpentry. Washington believed that these skills would enable African Americans to obtain jobs and lift themselves out of poverty. He cautioned African Americans

Booker T. Washington was born a slave, but he became one of the leading African-American educators and advocates for the rights of black people in America.

not to demand too much from whites but to coexist with them and be content to live separate lives. Washington once said "In all things that are purely social we can be as separate as the fingers, yet one as the hand in all things essential to mutual progress."

Washington's views were widely accepted by the white community because he seemed to pose no threat to them. However, he was fully aware of the discrimination that African Americans faced. Washington secretly paid for lawsuits to end discrimination and give African Americans the right to vote.

by a white mob. In fact, over the span of almost three decades, from 1890 to 1917, two or three African Americans were killed every week in the South by whites, who often accused them of crimes. Some were lynched, or dragged off and hanged by angry mobs without trial. Others were rapidly tried in front of all-white juries and then executed.

One leading southerner, Thomas Bailey, clearly described what whites wanted to accomplish by their treatment of African Americans: "The white race must dominate. . . . The Negro is inferior and will remain so. . . . No social equality. . . . No political equality." To ensure that African Americans did not achieve political equality in the South, they were prevented from voting. Although the Fourteenth Amendment guaranteed African Americans the right to vote, southern states found many ways to undercut the law. For example, black citizens who wanted to vote had to prove that they could read and understand the state constitution. When the blacks failed this test, which frequently happened, they were turned away and not allowed to vote. In truth, although they were not required to pass the same test, many white citizens would not have been able to read or understand the state constitutions either.

Although African Americans were prevented from achieving political power, a few managed to achieve economic success. They opened businesses such as insurance companies, banks, and funeral homes that served the African-American community. Some even built spacious houses for their families. However, these successful blacks often became the targets of white hatred. Riots broke out in Wilmington, North Carolina,

It's a Fact!

Between 1896 and 1904, the number of African-American voters in Louisiana dropped from 130,000 to 1,342. In neighboring Alabama, only 2 percent of the black citizens were voting.

in 1898 and in Atlanta, Georgia, in 1906. Middle-class blacks were killed and their homes destroyed. Many fled the cities.

Migration to the North

From 1910 to 1930, nearly 700,000 African Americans left the South and moved to northern cities, such as Chicago, New York, Pittsburgh, and Detroit. Many left the South to escape violence at the hands of white southerners. Others wanted to earn more money. In the steel mills of Pittsburgh and the new automobile plants in Detroit, black workers found higher-paying jobs.

Some African Americans in the North, however, were frustrated by the conditions they found there. Black workers faced discrimination in labor unions, which had been formed to represent employees in the workplace. Many unions refused to admit black workers.

Booker T. Washington and others had argued that African Americans must accept their place in society. A number of African Americans disagreed. In their eyes, this meant being second-class citizens and putting up with discrimination. Among these was William Edward Burghardt DuBois, known as W. E. B. DuBois. Born in Massachusetts in 1868, DuBois graduated from Harvard University and became a prominent historian. In his book *The Souls of Black Folk*, published in 1903, DuBois wrote: "Negroes must insist continually . . . that voting is necessary to modern manhood, that color discrimination is barbarism, and that black[s] . . . need education as well as white[s]." In 1909, DuBois became one of the founders of the National Association for the Advancement of Colored People (NAACP), which was committed to achieving equality for African Americans and ending discrimination.

Nine African-American soldiers from World War I prepare to return home in 1919. They all wear medals for bravery during combat.

African Americans found increased opportunities in the workplace with the outbreak of World War I in 1914. Before the war, immigrants from Europe had poured into the United States and filled many manufacturing jobs. These white immigrants were often hired ahead of African Americans. However, European immigration was interrupted by the war, opening up more opportunities for African Americans. In 1917, the United States entered the war, fighting with Britain, France, and Russia against Germany and Austria. Although some African Americans volunteered for the army, they were turned down for combat duty, just as they had been during the early part of the Civil

War. Instead, black soldiers were given jobs in training camps. Some African Americans joined French battle units. Needham Roberts and Henry Johnson, African-American members of the 369th French Infantry, were awarded a French medal, the Croix de Guerre, for bravery during a German attack in 1918.

More Discrimination

African Americans who returned from World War I found that little had changed for them in the United States. Although they had fought to defend the principles of democracy, these same principles did not seem to apply to them in their own country. In the South, African Americans still faced Jim Crow laws. In the North they faced resentment from whites, who saw African Americans competing for jobs and moving into white neighborhoods.

One organization that tried to prevent African Americans from improving their position in society was the Ku Klux Klan. Klan members, dressed in white robes and wearing hoods over their heads, terrorized African Americans throughout the South. They prevented them from voting, lynched black farmers, and burned their homes. With the onset of the Jim Crow laws, the activities of the Klan declined. After World War I, however, the Klan began to attract many new members, and their ranks rose to more than 2 million. To intimidate blacks, Klan members burned crosses in front of their homes and sometimes brutally beat them. In 1919 alone, the Klan carried out 78 lynchings of African Americans.

Racial hatred toward African Americans reached the crisis point in 1919 when race riots occurred in both northern and southern cities. In these riots, fueled by racial prejudice, violent clashes occurred between whites and blacks. A race riot in

Chicago lasted nearly two weeks, leaving 38 people dead and more than 500 injured.

White lynch mobs continued to murder African Americans throughout the 1920s. Many African Americans during this time felt that the best way to avoid trouble was to keep to themselves, so as not to invite the unwanted attention of racists, especially in the South. But this often meant missing out on opportunities for jobs or schooling. And for some African Americans, this was the same as accepting their second-class status in society.

Members of the Ku Klux Klan, a violently racist organization, wearing white hoods and robes gather at a 1965 rally before a flaming cross.

One of the few areas in which African Americans were able to freely express themselves was the arts. In New York City, which had a large African-American population, black musicians and artists began a cultural movement known as the Harlem Renaissance, named after the predominantly African-American section of New York City in which it was born. Jazz musicians such as Edward Kennedy "Duke" Ellington and singers such as Bessie Smith and Josephine Baker drew both white and black people by the thousands into clubs in Harlem to hear their music. Poet and playwright Langston Hughes and other African-American writers as well as actors such as Paul Robeson were also part of the Harlem Renaissance.

The cultural outburst of the Harlem Renaissance would be followed by a new chapter in the story of the descendants of the original Africans brought to the United States. In this era, they would achieve prominence not only in the arts but in many other areas of American society.

It's a Fact!

Between 1911 and 1930, almost 10 million immigrants entered the United States. Most of these newcomers came from Europe. Only about 15,000 were from Africa.

Opposite: *African-American students from Carolina A&T College take seats at a lunch counter reserved for whites only in 1960, in Greensboro, North Carolina. Similar protests called "sit-ins" took place throughout the South as African Americans insisted on equal rights with whites.*

Chapter Seven

Progress and Immigration

Civil Rights and Success

*States in which at least 10 percent of the
population was African American in 2002.*

The Great Depression

Beginning in October 1929, the United States suffered a
devastating economic collapse known as the Great
Depression. Many African Americans who had traveled north to
find new jobs in industry suddenly found themselves thrown out
of work along with millions of whites. Not surprisingly, unem-
ployment was even greater among African Americans than it was
for whites. In some cities, for instance, 70 percent of black
workers were unemployed. Immigration from Africa almost
came to a halt. Only 1,750 new African immigrants came to the
United States from 1931–1940.

President Franklin D. Roosevelt, elected in 1932, offered
Americans a plan that he called the New Deal. It included job

programs for the unemployed. Roosevelt also opened up jobs in his administration to thousands of African Americans.

In 1939, World War II broke out in Europe. The United States began providing military supplies to Great Britain and France. Suddenly there was a demand for more people to work in defense industries, building airplanes and manufacturing weapons. There was also more demand for people to join the military. African Americans, however, faced the same racial barriers they had in the past. But in 1941 President Roosevelt signed Executive Order 8802, which prohibited discrimination in any defense-related industry.

Later that year, the United States itself entered World War II after the Japanese attack on the American naval base at Pearl Harbor, Hawaii. Two million African Americans worked in defense industries during the war, while another million served in the armed forces. Black and white soldiers were generally enlisted in segregated military units.

Pressing for Change

African Americans returned home after World War II to face discrimination, just as they had after previous wars. They were frustrated by conditions in the United States that kept many of them from applying for good jobs, receiving the same education as whites, or living in the same communities. Led by the NAACP, African Americans began to increase the pressure for change during the 1950s.

In 1954, the NAACP won a landmark case before the Supreme Court, which struck down the separate-but-equal doctrine that had existed since the 1890s. Three years earlier, in Topeka, Kansas, Oliver Brown, with help from the NAACP, had sued the city's board of education. The purpose of the suit was to allow his daughter, Linda, to attend an all-white school instead of having to travel much farther from home to attend an inferior school for blacks. The case was brought before a federal court in Kansas by Thurgood Marshall, an African-American lawyer, who later became a Supreme Court Justice. Although that court ruled against Brown because both the black and white schools were considered equal, the judges stated "that segregation of colored children in public schools has a detrimental [negative] effect upon the colored children."

Based on this statement, Marshall and his team decided to take the case to the U.S. Supreme Court. In 1953, in a unanimous decision in the case of *Brown v. Board of Education of Topeka,* the Supreme Court stated: "We conclude, unanimously, that in the field of public education the doctrine of 'separate but equal' has no place. Separate educational facilities are inherently unequal." This decision by the Supreme Court signaled a major change in the position of African Americans throughout the United States.

Demanding Civil Rights

While the NAACP wanted desegregation (the elimination of "separate-but-equal" facilities) to begin immediately, the Supreme Court ruled that it should be carried out "with all deliberate speed." This meant that each state was free to proceed at its own pace to accomplish desegregation. In the South, organizations called White Citizens' Councils were formed to oppose desegregation, by violence if necessary.

African Americans refused to back down. In December 1955, Rosa Parks, a 43-year-old seamstress at a department store in Montgomery, Alabama, refused to move to the back of a bus and give up her seat to a white man. Police arrested Parks.

In support of Parks, the NAACP organized a bus boycott in Montgomery. During the boycott, African Americans refused to ride the city buses. Instead, they traveled in car pools, rode bicycles, or walked to work. As one woman remarked, "My feet is tired, but my soul is rested." The boycott was led by the Reverend Martin Luther King Jr. King, the pastor of the Dexter Avenue Baptist Church in Montgomery and a gifted public speaker. The boycott not only threatened to put the bus company out of business but also caused local merchants to lose money because fewer African Americans were coming into town. King was eventually arrested for violating an old state law against boycotts. His arrest was covered by the national news, bringing the plight of African Americans to the attention of the entire country and leading the Supreme Court to intervene. The Court ruled that Alabama's laws allowing segregation on buses were unconstitutional.

A group of angry white students jeer at Elizabeth Eckford as she walks to class at Central High School in Little Rock, Arkansas, in 1957.

The African-American movement for equal rights was gathering steam. In 1957, Governor Orval Faubus of Arkansas refused to permit black students to attend Central High School in Little Rock. When nine black teenagers tried to walk into Central High, they were threatened by an angry mob of white protesters. President Dwight Eisenhower sent in troops to protect the black teenagers. Over the next six years, the struggle for equal rights continued with a variety of protests, demonstrations, and other activities.

On August 28, 1963, the civil rights movement reached a crescendo when more than 200,000 people of all races rallied in Washington, D.C. In a speech delivered before the crowd, Martin Luther King Jr. proclaimed:

> *I have a dream today. . . . From every mountainside, let freedom ring. And when this happens and when we allow freedom to ring, when we let it ring from every village and every hamlet, from every state and every city, we will be able to speed up that day when all God's children . . . will be able to join hands and sing in the words of the old Negro spiritual: "Free at last, Free at last. Thank God Almighty, we are free at last!"*

Civil Rights Legislation

In 1963, President John F. Kennedy introduced new civil rights legislation. The bill called for an end to discrimination in public facilities, desegregation of schools, and equal opportunity for African Americans in employment. Kennedy was assassinated in Dallas, Texas, on November 22 that year, before the new Civil Rights Act could be passed. After Vice

President Lyndon Johnson succeeded to the presidency, he led the effort to pass the bill, which became law in 1964.

Meanwhile, black leaders were engaged in a program to increase voter registration among African Americans throughout the South. They realized that African Americans had to be permitted to vote in order to elect officials who would enforce the civil rights laws and prevent discrimination.

In 1965, President Johnson led the fight to pass a Voting Rights Act in Congress. Under the act, federal officials could be sent into local districts to ensure that the registrars of voters did not discriminate against African Americans. As a result of the Voting Rights Act, more and more African Americans voted in local and statewide elections.

Black Muslim leader Malcolm X holds up a newspaper for the crowd to see during a rally in New York City in 1963.

The efforts to provide equality for African Americans were only beginning. During the summers of the mid-1960s, race riots broke out in both northern and southern cities across America. An investigation into the riots revealed that African Americans were still encountering segregation in housing and employment. When Martin Luther King was assassinated by a white man in Memphis, Tennessee, on April 4, 1968, blacks rioted in more than 100 cities across the nation. As a result, Congress passed a new Civil Rights Act, prohibiting racial discrimination in housing.

As native born African Americans gained more freedoms, a new group of immigrants began entering the United States from Africa. The number of African immigrants jumped from about 175 per year from 1931 to 1940 to 750 per year in the next decade. The total almost doubled to about 1,400 per year from 1951 to 1960. This trend continued as the number of African immigrants more than doubled again to almost 29,000 from 1961 to 1970. Although the number of new immigrants from Africa was still less than one percent of the overall total of immigrants entering the United States, these increases marked the beginning of a new era of African immigration. ▨

Opposite: *Two people dressed in traditional African clothing examine the Kwanzaa display in the House of Kwanzaa at the Saint Louis, Missouri, convention center in 1997. Kwanzaa is a celebration of African culture and community begun in 1966 by a group of African Americans who wanted to remember and celebrate their African heritage.*

Chapter Eight

A New Era of Immigration

African Immigrants in Their New Land

New Immigrants

During the 1970s and 1980s, African Americans made important gains in politics, business, and education. During this time, African Americans also attended college in greater numbers. By the mid-1990s, more than 37 percent of black students who graduated from high school went to college, up from 7 percent in 1960. More African Americans also started businesses and reached the executive levels in large corporations. Some moved out of the cities into previously all-white suburbs, taking advantage of their higher incomes and federal laws that prevented segregation in housing.

These advances for African Americans contributed to an increase in the number of people who immigrated to the United States from Africa. For the first time, large numbers of Africans came to America by their own choice, to take advantage of the opportunities that awaited them.

Between 1900 and 1970, only 74,800 African immigrants had arrived in the United States. However, this number grew to almost 64,000 in the next decade alone from 1971 to 1980. At first, many Africans traveled to the United States only to obtain a better education than was available in their home countries. Africans educated in the United States returned to their own countries hoping to participate in the newly independent governments and to develop the local economies.

During the 1960s, many African governments were taken over by dictators. In addition, corruption hurt the economies of these new nations. As a result, jobs were scarce. These political and economic problems in Africa served as a powerful force that pushed African immigrants from their homelands to the United States. Job opportunities in major cities such as

New York, Atlanta, Chicago, and Los Angeles, acted as a strong force pulling in many African immigrants. The 1980s brought more than 150,000 new African immigrants to the United States. In addition, new U.S. immigration laws encouraged Africans to move to North America. The 1990 Immigration Act, for example, allowed up to 50,000 additional new African immigrants to come to the United States. As a result, in 2000, an estimated 92,000 African immigrants lived in New York City. By 2003, 200,000 African immigrants lived in Atlanta.

In those cities the newcomers were welcomed by earlier immigrants. Historian John Arthur, in his book *Invisible Sojourners,* a history of 20th-century African immigration, explains that immigrants in cities such as Washington, D.C., and Atlanta have established mutual aid societies to help recent immigrants become accustomed to their new way of life in the United States. Approximately 75 percent of these immigrants have attended college, while almost 90 percent have a high school diploma. This is a higher percentage than the number of non-immigrant African Americans graduating from high school.

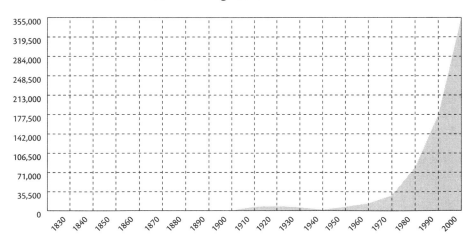

African Immigration to America

A woman carrying an Ethiopian flag representing the United African Movement marches in Harlem during the 29th annual African American Day Parade in 1997 in New York City. The parade promotes unity in the African-American community.

In the 1990s, more than 40,000 immigrants came from Ethiopia, while others emigrated from Nigeria, Mali, Senegal, and the Ivory Coast. Some were trying to escape dangerous political conditions; others were seeking better jobs in the United States. Many of these immigrants started new businesses. They opened restaurants and grocery stores featuring African foods, as well as taxi services and travel agencies. Nightclubs also sprang up, featuring African singers and musicians. Many other immigrants filled lower-paying positions, driving taxicabs, working in restaurants, or picking fruits and vegetables on commercial farms.

No matter how much they earn, however, many African immigrants send some money back home to help support relatives in Africa. And even those who have low-paying jobs do not plan to return to their homelands. As one immigrant put it: "Leaving to go back home would amount to an admission of failure, a disappointment to relatives. Better to endure in silence than pack and go home."

Africa in America

Like millions of immigrants before them, many African immigrants arrive in New York City. And just like their predecessors from Europe, these immigrants want to live and work near other people who speak the same languages and share the same customs. Many Africans have found such a place in the neighborhood of Clifton on Staten Island, one of the five boroughs that make up New York City. Easy access to the many job opportunities in New York makes this a logical place to live.

However, what attracts many African immigrants from the West African countries of Nigeria and Liberia are the African restaurants, night clubs, and stores that line Targee Street in the heart of Clifton. Both men and women can be seen on the street dressed in African tribal gowns and headwear. Anthony Idow who immigrated to the United States from Nigeria summed up his attraction to this neighborhood, "This is the way we lead our life back home."

Success Stories

Many African immigrants have overcome great hardships in their transition to a successful life in the United States. One such immigrant from Ethiopia, a war-torn African nation, is Tesfay Sebahtu. In the 1970s, when he was a young child, his mother managed to take him out of Ethiopia to nearby Sudan, where they lived in Port Sudan, on the Red Sea. Sebahtu spoke a little English and eventually was able to emigrate to the United States in 1981. He lived in a group home run by a charitable organization outside Washington, D.C. There he met other refugees from Ethiopia. "We all got attached to each other in the house," he recalled. "We were just like brothers and sisters." Sebahtu attended high school and eventually enrolled at the University of Maryland, where he graduated in 1993 with a degree in electrical engineering. Meanwhile, his mother and sisters had also obtained visas and come to the United States.

Who Are African Americans?

Although most black Americans prefer to call themselves African Americans, they do not all think that recent African immigrants are entitled to use the term. Some American-born blacks believe that only people born in the United States who share the heritage of slavery and oppression should be called "African Americans." Many recent immigrants such as Abdulaziz Kamus, an immigrant from Ethopia, do not agree. He sums up the feelings of many African immigrants when he says, "I am African and I am an American citizen; am I not African-American?" Other immigrants have adopted the use of their home country to help distinguish them from native-born African Americans. They call themselves Ethiopian Americans or Nigerian Americans.

*A young African-American girl is cheered after reciting the poem
"I Am Your Child" in Arabic, Swahili, and English during the Annual
Day of Prayer for the African Burial Ground in New York City in 2003.*

Other immigrants have gained success by nurturing their African heritage. Khadija Sow is an African immigrant from Senegal, who arrived in the United States during the 1990s. She opened a restaurant in Brooklyn, New York. One of her most popular dishes is Thiebu Djeun, a fish stew with rice. "Our traditional cuisine is in high demand among single African males who were brought up with the idea that a man's place is not in the kitchen," Sow explained. Another tradition in Senegal and other African countries is hair braiding, which became very fashionable in the United States. Aminata Dia, an immigrant from Senegal, opened a hair salon in the 1990s.

Other African immigrants practice traditional crafts. Habi Bah, from Mali, works as a travel agent in New York City. She has many clients among African immigrants who sell their crafts in major cities throughout the United States.

Some African immigrants excel in professional sports. Dikembe Mutombo, for example, left his home in the Democratic Republic of the Congo in the late 1980s to attend college at Georgetown University in Washington, D.C. Now a professional basketball player, Mutombo received the National Basketball Association (NBA) Community Assist Award in 2003. He was given the award for his work with the United Nations and the NBA's Africa 100 Camp. As part of the camp, Mutombo helped teach basketball to a hundred leading young players from 19 African countries. As he explained, "As an African who was born and raised in the Democratic Republic of the Congo, I count myself fortunate to have the opportunity to live in two very different worlds."

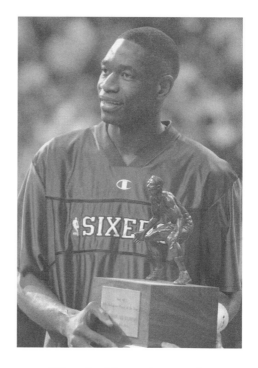

Dikembe Mutombo was the NBA's Defensive Player of the Year in 2001.

Despite their success, African immigrants have faced problems adjusting to American society. The most difficult is racial prejudice. According to historian John Arthur, these immigrants report that they are often looked down on by whites, who treat them just as they do other African Americans. Nevertheless, African immigrants are proud of their heritage. In their homes, they continue to prepare African dishes, such as chicken and okra stew and peanut butter or palm nut soup. Their stores sell African clothing, music, and jewelry. Some of the clothing styles, jewelry, and foods from Africa have become popular among white Americans.

> ## It's a Fact!
>
> In 2003, the American Broadcasting Company and the *Washington Post* conducted a poll and found that 48 percent of blacks preferred to be called "African American," 35 percent referred to themselves as "black," and 17 percent thought either term was appropriate.

Africans have a long history of coming to America. For almost two centuries, Africans were brought to America as slaves. Even after slavery was abolished, African Americans experienced discrimination in every aspect of society. Because of the harsh conditions of slavery and discrimination, few Africans voluntarily immigrated to the United States until the last quarter of the 20th century.

In spite of the many hardships they have endured, native-born African Americans have made extraordinary contributions to American society. They are a vital part of the fabric of American life. As more and more African immigrants come to America, they bring with them the same hopes for a better future that motivated other immigrant groups to seek a new life in the United States, and they are already making their own contributions to their new homeland.

Time Line of Africans in America

1619	First black Africans arrive in Virginia.
1770	The African-American population of the 13 colonies exceeds 400,000.
1739	Slaves revolt in Stono Rebellion in South Carolina.
1775–1781	African Americans serve as soldiers in American Revolution.
1787	The Constitutional Convention agrees to continue international slave trade until 1808.
1800	Slaves revolt in Virginia.
1803	United States makes Louisiana Purchase, increasing land suitable for plantations and slave labor.
1803–1807	South Carolina imports 40,000 African slaves.
1820	The U.S. government records show only one voluntary African immigrant.
1831	Slaves led by Nat Turner revolt in Virginia.
1842	Harriet Jacobs escapes from slavery to the North; becomes a leader of Underground Railroad.
1850	Congress passes Fugitive Slave Law.
1859	Abolitionist John Brown leads raid on Harpers Ferry Arsenal in West Virginia.
1861–1865	African Americans fight in Civil War.
1865	Thirteenth Amendment ending slavery is passed.
1867	Reconstruction begins in the South.
1868	The Fourteenth Amendment giving African Americans the right to vote and run for elected office becomes law.

1870s	The southern states pass Jim Crow laws enforcing segregation of African Americans.
1896	Segregation is upheld by U.S. Supreme Court in *Plessy v. Ferguson.*
1906	Race riots break out in Atlanta, Georgia.
1910–1930	More than 700,000 African Americans migrate from South to North, and 15,000 African immigrants come to the United States.
1917–1918	African Americans fight in World War I.
1920s	The Harlem Renaissance, a major African-American cultural movement, begins in New York City.
1941–1945	African Americans fight in World War II.
1954	The Supreme Court reverses *Plessy v. Ferguson,* ending school segregation in *Brown v. Board of Education of Topeka, Kansas.*
1963	The Reverend Martin Luther King Jr. leads sit-in demonstrations for civil rights in Montgomery, Alabama, and march on Washington, D.C.
1964	Congress passes the Civil Rights Act.
1965	Congress passes the Voting Rights Act.
1968	The Reverend Martin Luther King Jr. is assassinated in Memphis, Tennessee.
1970–1980	Voluntary African immigration exceeds one percent of the total immigrants for the first time.
1976	Congressional representative Barbara Jordan becomes the first African-American woman to speak at the Democratic National Convention.
1989	L. Douglas Wilder (Virginia) becomes first African American elected governor since Reconstruction.
1990–2000	More than 200,000 immigrants from various countries in Africa come to the United States.

Glossary

artisan Person skilled at a craft, such as a blacksmith or butcher.

culture The language, arts, traditions, and beliefs of a society.

democracy Government by the majority rule of the people.

discrimination Targeting a particular group of people with laws or actions, often because of their race.

emigrate Leave one's homeland to live in another country.

export Send goods out of a country to sell in another.

heritage Cultural tradition handed down from generation to generation.

immigrate Come to a foreign country to live.

import Bring goods from foreign countries into another to sell.

labor union Organization that fights for workers' rights such as better pay and working conditions.

pidgin English Language used by slaves that was a combination of various African languages and English.

prejudice Negative opinion formed without just cause.

racist Someone who believes that one race is better than others.

refugee Someone who flees a place for safety reasons, especially to another country.

Reconstruction Program started by Congress after the Civil War to enforce equal rights for African Americans in the South.

segregation Separating groups of people from each other, especially according to race.

spiritual Deeply religious song based on verses from the Bible.

Further Reading

BOOKS

Ashabranner, Brent, and Jennifer Ashabranner. *The New African Americans*. North Haven, Conn.: Shoe String Press, 1999.

Asgedom, Maui. *Of Beetles and Angels: A Boy's Remarkable Journey from a Refugee Camp to Harvard*. New York: Little, Brown, 2002.

Haskins, James. *Out of Darkness: The Story of Blacks Moving North, 1890–1940*. Tarrytown, N.Y.: Marshall Cavendish, 2000.

McKissack, Patricia, and Frederick McKissack. *Rebels Against Slavery: American Slave Revolts*. New York: Scholastic Press, 1996.

Sawyer, Kem Knapp. *The Underground Railroad in American History*. Springfield, N.J.: Enslow, 1997.

Tucker, Philip Thomas. *From Auction Block to Glory: The African American Experience*. New York: Metro Books, 1998.

Wexler, Sanford. *An Eyewitness History of the Civil Rights Movement*. New York: Checkmark Books, 1999.

WEB SITES

The African American Mosaic. "A Library of Congress Resource Guide for the Study of Black History & Culture" URL: http://www.loc.gov/exhibits/african/intro.html. Updated on October 14, 2004.

Library of Congress: American Memory. "Immigration . . . African." URL: http://memory.loc.gov/learn/features/immig/alt/african.html. Updated on October 14, 2004.

National Park Service. "Our Shared History: African American Heritage." URL: http://www.cr.nps.gov/aahistory. Downloaded on October 14, 2004.

Index

Page numbers in *italics* indicate photographs. Page numbers followed by *m* indicate maps. Page numbers followed by *g* indicate glossary entries. Page numbers in **boldface** indicate box features.